BLENDED FAMILY

A Guide for Stepparents

Seven Unsuspecting Attitudes
That Are Seriously Toxic to Stepfamilies

BLENDED FAMILY

A Guide for Stepparents

Seven Unsuspecting Attitudes
That Are Seriously Toxic to Stepfamilies

Andrea Campbell

Pocket Learner Publishing

© Copyright Andrea Campbell 2022 - All rights reserved.

The content contained in this book may not be reproduced, duplicated or transmitted without direct written permission from the author or publisher.

Under no circumstances will any blame or legal responsibility be held against the publisher, or author, for any damages, reparation, or monetary loss due to the information contained within this book; either directly or indirectly. You are responsible for your own choices, actions, and results.

Legal Notice:

This book is copyright protected and is only for personal use. You cannot amend, distribute, sell, use, quote or paraphrase any part, or the content within this book, without the consent of the author or publisher.

Disclaimer Notice:

Please note the information contained in this text is for educational and entertainment purposes only. All effort has been executed to present accurate, up-to-date, and reliable, complete information. No warranties of any kind are declared or implied. Readers acknowledge that the author is not engaging in the rendering of legal, financial, medical, or professional advice. The content within this book has been derived from various sources. Please consult a licensed professional before attempting any techniques outlined in this book.

By reading this document, the reader agrees that under no circumstances is the author responsible for any losses, direct or indirect, which are incurred as a result of the use of the information contained within this document, including, but not limited to, errors, omissions, or inaccuracies.

Inspirational quotes – Andrea Campbell intellectual property

Pocket Learner Publishing

ISBN: 978-1-914997-05-1 - (sc)
ISBN: 978-1-914997-06-8 - (hc)

I would like to thank my family —

Richmond and Shari

for their inspiration, understanding

and love.

A Note from the Author

I need your help!

If you enjoy the book and want to support our mission to make a difference, here are ways you can help:

1. **Buy a paper copy.** Thirty percent of the proceeds from sales go to Camptys Foundation – a non-profit which provides support for families caring for children with special needs in developing countries. (See more at camptys.org). You can buy the book on Amazon and at most places where books are sold.

2. **Give a copy.** Find someone who could benefit from the content in this book. This includes stepparents, divorcees and adult children in stepfamilies.

3. **Write a review** – we'd appreciate it very much if you could leave a review on the site where you bought the book. This helps our books to rank and become more visible to other readers who could benefit from the content.

Table of Contents

PREFACE ix
INTRODUCTION 1
Chapter 1 - BUREAUCRACY 5
   Rules and Differently-abled Children 6
   Adaptability in Blended Families 7
   Imperfect Stepparents 9
Chapter 2 - LAMBASTING 11
   Communication Issues 13
   Offence and Punishment 15
Chapter 3 - UNFORGIVENESS 17
   Setting the Stage 18
   Letting Go 19
   Changing Faces 21
Chapter 4 - NEPOTISM 23
   The Pet Phenomenon 24
   Collateral Damage 27
Chapter 5 - DEARTH 29
   The Scarcity Mindset 31
   The Concept of Money 32
   Additional Expenses 34
   An Abundance Mindset 35
Chapter 6 - ENNUI 37
   Strategies for Tackling Boredom 38
   The Beauty of Creativity 40

Time for Love.. 41
Chapter 7 - RETICENCE............................... 43
　　When Silence isn't Golden................................. 44
　　Communication Woes 46
CONCLUSION 49
RESOURCES 57
ABOUT THE AUTHOR 58

PREFACE

There are certain dynamics to consider and process when two families join. Getting used to the role of stepparent can be stressful and adjustment takes time. Combining two families under one roof can prove challenging; even for the most prepared, there will be periods of discomfort and pain in the process.

Children are affected when their original family breaks up and a blended family is formed. They find themselves having to adjust to a new parent and new rules. They may express their frustration with this process through behavioral or emotional outbursts. Children may struggle with feelings about a new stepparent and feel unloved or feel as if they do not fit. These dynamics affect the new stepfamily. Stepparents will find themselves having to balance emotions with duty.

When you consider the presence of other parties, such as birth families, grandparents, former partners and family friends, you find that a range of factors can infiltrate the home and cause added stress and uncertainty to the family unit. When faced with this mish-mash of factors, stepparents often make the error of tightening the reins in hopes of reducing or eliminating outside influence and restoring order to their home.

Overparenting is when parents are excessive in their attempts to manage their kids' lives. While you might be allowing them to make decisions and have autonomy, you may still be hovering about incessantly. Even if you have only the best intentions for your children, overparenting or micromanaging them will likely do more harm than good. Here are signs that you are micromanaging your kids:

1. Whenever they have friends over, you fuss about every little thing, such as what they eat, what they're wearing or what they should do for fun. Leave them alone. You may be interrupting their fun.

2. You arbitrate without their invitation or permission if you hear that they've had small arguments with friends or siblings. This action results in a dispute between you and your child because they feel that you are interfering.

3. You become too obsessive about the food they eat. In your desire to ensure that your children eat healthily, you control what they eat. Eventually, your relationship with them becomes unhealthy.

4. You find yourself eavesdropping on their conversations with others or checking emails and text messages. This action is going overboard with your parenting—set boundaries for yourself.

Unless there is a clear and imminent danger to their lives, you should stop micromanaging your children. A blended family is complicated enough without adding such drama to your relationship with your stepchildren. This can also happen when you micromanage your special child. Though this child may need supervision, you still need to allow them their space to develop their imagination and autonomy.

I have written this book to show that there is another way. Fighting fire with fire is never a good idea; it is always better to grab a bucket of water, even if it's against everything you believe. Ultimately, your home is where you should feel most secure. To achieve this, you must take steps to promote peace in your stepfamily.

WHAT LOVE IS

Love says yes and love says no

Love holds on and love lets go

Love is being, love is doing

Love is really understanding.

—Andrea Campbell

INTRODUCTION

Blended families are often the result of a breakdown of the original family or the death of a parent. It is understandable, therefore, that children experience intense and sometimes overwhelming feelings of anger, disappointment, and sadness. Some experience grief, guilt, and anxiety, leading to depression and feelings of insecurity. When a parent remarries or moves in with a new partner, children face further threats to their sense of security and stability.

Some seventy-five to eighty per cent of divorced parents in the USA remarry. This means that many people face the need to adjust to this significant transition.

Every parent of a blended family aspires for their child and their new partner to get along. If the partner also has children, the new couple will hope the children bond quickly so that the new family can settle down and function normally. It takes time for a blended family to stabilize, and it can be upsetting when there is misery in the household despite the adults' best attempts to make things work. Sometimes, in despair, parents make mistakes in the approaches they adopt to achieve cohesion and happiness in their new family unit. Unfortunately, the failure to address issues, or the hope that they will simply disappear on their own, rarely yields positive results. If they don't get the dynamics right, parents will struggle to maintain a happy and healthy household. In many cases they fail and become yet another statistic of unsuccessful blended families.

I have written this book to help stepfamilies navigate this challenging but potentially enriching role. A successful blended family takes more than the desire or intent to make it work. Stepparents must adopt and apply a range of skills to keep their families together while maintaining flexibility. The seven elements presented in this book are often overlooked or are lost in the noise of contemporary society, where parents are busy juggling the different facets of their lives. However, if you pay attention to the elements I have outlined, the difference will be noticeable, and your family will be on its way to finding peace.

I've dedicated my professional life to supporting parents of children with special needs from varying backgrounds. Having grown up in a blended family, and now being the mom and stepmom of a family with a special child, I have seen how this unique family type, also referred to as a stepfamily, can produce happy, resilient, and confident children with or without special needs.

I have also seen how quickly things can go wrong. This is often because of unconscious attitudes which can become embedded and adversely impact the stepfamily. Attention to these seemingly minor issues can make a world of difference in any family.

Working with families from different cultures has enriched my outlook on blended family life. I have had opportunities to live and work in several countries, and I have learned that one size does not fit all. There's no single winning formula for building a happy blended family, especially when that family is caring for a differently-abled child.

Blending families can be a complicated and challenging transition to navigate. The observations I have made throughout years of professional work with families and personal experience contribute to the information I have presented in this book. This non-traditional checklist outlines critical factors that, when routinely overlooked and unchecked, can damage families and deny them the peaceful existence they desire and deserve. I hope to encourage personal introspection and reflection, followed by concerted action to initiate and consolidate change. Stepparents should discuss the factors with each other in honest conversations to explore how they could improve their experience, starting with small sustainable steps that benefit each family member.

The seven attitudes I present spell the word BLUNDER because, in my mind, that is precisely what stepparents do when they adopt these attitudes or fail to address them.

This is a concise text for the parental figure needing a quick read. I want to draw your attention to my full-length book, "Blended and Special", available wherever books are sold. The in-depth book is a compilation of strategies for issues confronting blended families as they navigate their way in the world of stepparenting children with special needs.

Also available is the book: "The Pocket Learner–Special Needs Education," which presents a unique framework to empower families of children with special needs to support their children's cognitive and physical development. This book is a comprehensive guide to caring for children with special needs from the very early years up until adulthood.

I hope you find the material in this book insightful. So let's dive right in!

Chapter 1

BUREAUCRACY

You can do a good thing but it may not be the right thing.
—*Andrea Campbell*

Rules are essential in every sphere of life. We live by rules, many of which we implement ourselves and gladly follow. For example, you can't just approach someone in the street and hug them. This is an extreme example, but is it universal? Why don't we do it? Where is the rule written down that prohibits this sort of behavior? It is written nowhere, and yet we abide by it! Adults in a family unit often establish and implement strict orders and rules, which weigh down the family, causing undue stress and misery. This sort of bureaucracy is damaging to families. Insisting on officialdom, procedures, and strict rules creates unnecessary stress in your stepfamily.

All families have rules–spoken or unspoken. However, rules are generally more noticeable in stepfamilies because, as two families merge, they combine their traditions, routines, and habits.

Early in the union, there must be discussions between the parents about the rules in your home as you raise your children. These may differ based on the home culture where the child lived before the stepfamily was formed. For example, a child raised in a particular religion may want to attend religious events, which may not apply to the other children. Notwithstanding the existence of rules and levels of authority in the household, a stepparent should be primarily a friend or confidant, not a disciplinarian. Biological parents should remain primarily responsible for discipline until a solid bond and trust have been well-established.

Rules and Differently-abled Children

Children with special needs, especially when they have cognitive disabilities, often do not follow the rules. Stepparents must find creative ways to introduce the rules to these children to aid their learning and encourage them to establish appropriate behavior. For example, my daughter had the poor habit of taking food from the plate of others while sitting at the dining-room table. She did not consider this to be unacceptable. As a family, we consistently discouraged this behavior and did not yield to her desires. Soon enough, she learned she had to focus on the food on her own plate instead of other people's. As is the case in the neuro-typical child, teaching children with special needs is a constant undertaking.

A child with special needs who is non-verbal requires additional latitude as they may not be able to articulate their feelings, including any pain or illness they may be experiencing. While you want them to conform and treat them as you do any other child, you must remember that they are living with a disability and, in some cases, may have complex needs. These circumstances demand extra patience and understanding.

Adaptability in Blended Families

Even as your family works to establish consistent expectations, some rules may have to be broken for the sake of peace. If a child capable of making his bed doesn't do it one day, it is not the end of the world. Let it slide if he doesn't want to eat with the family today. Yes, we want all these social rules to be followed, but what will happen if they aren't? Would you prefer a child who flaunts the rules from time to time or a child who decides to run away or turn to strangers for what they see as a loving environment? The child will eventually yield to your instructions as they feel respected, loved, and understood. They must not be bombarded with strict rules. That is not to say they will become perfect; it only means they will work with you more often. Little by little, both sides will make concessions to achieve greater peace in your household. Slackening some rules also reduces stress and helps you save energy for critical issues.

An adaptable stepfamily will change as circumstances evolve. Though each family member may have set tasks, there needs to be a measure of flexibility that will not destabilize the family if any member falls out of line. While parents must maintain structure, they should avoid being autocratic or emotionally abusive.

Homes with excessive bureaucracy often have a clinical look, with a specific place and time for everything. Mealtimes are at the same time every day, and the menus may be set for different days. The children may be required to eat in silence unless their parents invite them to speak. These families may pride themselves on maintaining structure and instilling good manners in their children. In those situations, the children do not feel free to share information such as the day's events or any concerns they may have, and the stepfamily misses out on chances to bond. Worse, they may miss out on opportunities to save their children from making unnecessary and costly mistakes. The lines of communication must remain open to access the information you need to keep your children safe and address emerging issues early.

When stepparents maintain a household with exceedingly rigid rules, they risk becoming distant, imposing figures, and children may seek closeness or affection from any available adult. These circumstances put them at risk to abuse as they turn to people outside the family unit for what they see as love.

Notwithstanding the suggestion to avoid being overly strict with the children in your stepfamily, it is important not to swing too far to the other extreme where families become chaotic. Peace doesn't thrive in chaos. In chaotic families, there are few rules, or existing rules may change at a whim based on the parents' mood. Also, unacceptable behavior may warrant punishment at one moment and not the next. There is no set place for objects in these households, and family members can eat when and where they like.

While some people may think they are happy in chaos, that is not the case for most. The desired position is somewhere in-between a highly bureaucratic approach and chaos. Together with their children, stepparents must find the right balance that works for their family unit.

Imperfect Stepparents

Stepparents often experience guilt due to the failure of previous relationships. There is no reason to feel guilty if you gave it your best. Families, irrespective of their makeup, are not perfect. If you think you failed in your former relationship, see this new relationship as an opportunity to get it right. Don't dampen the environment in your home by being too rigid. Instead, strive for joy in your family unit. Believe you can succeed even if the way forward is unclear.

Parents in traditional family structures don't have perfect lives, irrespective of what outside appearances might suggest. Parenting is hard–whether biological or stepkids. When one or more children are differently abled, there are even more demands on the family. Try to go with the flow sometimes, and do your best. If you're honest with yourself and your partner, you'll put the children's needs first and let go of perfect. You'll get there in the end.

Don't pressure yourself, your partner, or the children to live up to an ideal you created or to which you aspire. For example, if your stepkids don't want to call you Mom or Dad, don't take it personally. I understand that you may feel hurt since you are playing the role of a parent, but at the end of the day, you are not their biological parent and therefore being acknowledged as Mom or Dad might never happen. That's the reality, be at peace with it.

Key points:

- Some children find it challenging to follow the rules, and it is up to stepparents to be creative and flexible.
- Order is essential, but avoid overkill if you wish to reduce or eliminate stress in your stepfamily.
- Prioritize peace and joy over rules and order in your stepfamily.

Chapter 2

LAMBASTING

Learn to ignore the subject but pass the course
—Andrea Campbell

Closely linked to strictly enforced rules in the home is the issue of discipline. This subject is essential in bringing up children to function effectively in society. It is, therefore, not about the *what*; instead, it is about *how* children are corrected, taught, and trained. But, again, this is not an either-or situation; there is a need to balance both.

Children with special needs too must be subjected to discipline. Do not assume that the child will not understand or assimilate instructions because they have a disability.

In my earlier example of my daughter dipping into the plates of others around the table, most parents would be quick to rebuke their neurotypical children but perhaps not their child with special needs. Both children must receive teaching, and it is up to parents to determine the level and method of engagement with each child. I grew up in a blended family, and I think I would have responded better if kinder forms of correction had been employed.

Competition is rife for our children's attention. They are exposed to a wide array of risks, so there is much they can keep hidden from their parents. If we consistently rebuke them, our attitude will adversely impact their happiness in the home, forcing them to close down and find solace elsewhere.

When I was fourteen years old, I ran away from home and went to a friend's house. I had seen how well her mother treated her. My mother, in contrast, was an extreme disciplinarian who grasped at every opportunity to punish me even when I was not guilty of anything. I felt, therefore, that I could not do anything right. I was broken, had no self-esteem, and if a stranger had appeared and beckoned me, "Come," I would have complied without a second thought. Luckily, it turned out right in the end.

My easy-going stepfather dared not intervene as my mother rained terror on me. I returned home eventually, and my mother's behavior improved noticeably.

Don't fall into the trap of comparing your family to other blended families. Appearances can be deceiving; no one has it all together. Instead, concentrate on your family, let things happen organically, and don't be preoccupied with the sentiments of others.

Communication Issues

Improve your communication skills. If communication within your blended family is poor, you'll feel like you are not in control and lambaste your children even more. Instead, it is best to define boundaries, sustain open communication and build bridges where these are needed. Don't yield to the temptation to yell at or curse at the children. An angry household is not a happy household. When you yell, you teach your children to behave likewise when faced with challenging circumstances. Don't be surprised if they raise their voices in return when it was you who taught them the technique.

Raising children in a blended family can be frustrating and overwhelming. It can test your endurance irrespective of how patient you are. There will be moments when you doubt your ability to hold the family together, and, without intending to, you explode and rain terror on your stepchildren and partner. It can be painful to be unacknowledged or disrespected despite all you do as a stepparent.

Children often test their parents, but you acquire valuable experience and expertise to take you to the next level when you pass the test. True strength lies within, and you'll find it if you consciously reach for it.

There will be no growth if everything is easy and there is no challenge.

As parents, we have to dot the I's and cross the T's of others as we punctuate our way through life, adding value to those we care for. When you are entrusted with raising a child with any form of impairment, you embark on a journey that takes you out of your comfort zone and transforms you into a person of value not only to your family but to society. It may not feel like it, but these tests hone your skills for broader impact. The key is believing in the possibilities and the processes necessary to bring them to fruition, even before they can become a reality.

Include the children in decision-making and make them accountable and responsible for distinctive roles within the family unit. If things become overwhelming, take some time with your partner one-on-one and work it out. You are in a partnership and must find time to support each other for the sake of a happy stepfamily. When you adopt a collaborative approach to discipline, you'll reduce your stress levels, the challenges will become easier to overcome, and minor hiccups will have no way of escalating into issues of significant proportion.

And while we're at it, I must mention the need to avoid using swear words in the presence of and for addressing children. Some stepparents find the use of swear words funny and consider it harmless. Some even mentioned that the children understand that they should not repeat curse words. I believe this approach is short-sighted and erroneous. Why would you teach your child lessons that they cannot utilize freely? We may not see them as lessons, but that's exactly what they are.

Offence and Punishment

Irrespective of how unruly your children may be, they do not deserve extreme punishment or abuse. They will never understand or welcome abusive or extreme punitive behavior from their parents or stepparents. No one enjoys constant battering, whether it be verbally or physically. We can destroy our children's ability to experience joy, making them develop hatred for us.

A destroyed self-esteem is of no value to anyone. It creates an excuse for the child to misbehave and disrupt the family unit. Trust breaks down, and love goes out the window. The stepchildren will no longer be your allies and they will grab any opportunity to unseat you. This situation is perilous when a threatening ex-partner is waiting in the wings.

It is said that honesty is the best policy and whether you agree with that sentiment or not, you can at least agree that honesty with oneself is a good policy. That being said, let's acknowledge that sometimes our anger has nothing to do with the child but is due to our frustrations with life. We juggle personal issues with external factors which often make us fearful or anxious. The child's unacceptable behavior is often "the straw that breaks the camel's back." Once we recognize this, and take note for the next time we are angry, we will behave differently, and even if our kindness is taken for weakness we'll be well on our way to having a more peaceful existence.

If you are always bitter and angry, you will put a strain on your family and repel the very people you are trying to love. You will also damage your friendships and other relationships with your own hands, leaving you alone to pick up your pieces.

If you're struggling to connect as a blended family, consider getting professional help. No one is born a stepmom or stepdad; it takes learning and time. You may have unresolved feelings from prior experiences—divorce and separation, death in the family, abuse or neglect. These feelings can come to the fore and overwhelm a family if the parents have not laid them to rest. They inspire negativity, cause conflict, and stir up anger. An honest conversation with an unconnected and objective professional can help your stepfamily heal from issues of the past.

Key Points:

- Anger can destroy your children's joy, and that will make them develop hatred for you.

- Be the parent that empowers, lifts, and encourages—even if your actions are not reciprocated, your peace of mind depends on it.

- Endeavor to ensure that your actions uplift your children and that these actions are not soul-destroying.

Chapter 3

UNFORGIVENESS

You don't have to flex your muscles in order to win; learn to drop it, leave it, and let it go.

—Andrea Campbell

One of the qualities that destroy us human beings is our inability or unwillingness to forgive. When we hold on to past pain, we hurt ourselves and others. Unforgiveness is a failure to let go and forgive people who have offended you. It is characterized by bitterness, resentment, and animosity and may be accompanied by a hunger for punishment or restitution. This state of affairs causes emotional and mental distress.

Children have parents for a reason. We are there to guide and protect, teach and inspire. Children sometimes make mistakes or break the rules—that's what children do. In their eagerness to explore and make sense of the world, they often venture steps in the wrong direction. We cannot guard against or protect them from every single mistake. Our role is to be there before, during, and after these steps have been taken.

With all the pressures and life challenges we encounter, we cannot afford to hang on to negative baggage. So, for example, don't keep reminding Johnny that he made the same mistake last week and perhaps the week before, and here he is doing it again. In your mind, you think you are saying, "Please stop doing that," while in his mind, he hears, "you are stupid and useless, Johnny."

Setting the Stage

All children misbehave at times; it is called being a child. Your stepchild may react to the change in family life by misbehaving more often than is acceptable. Remember that their whole world has changed, and change is often uncomfortable. They need stability, reassurance and routine—which includes boundaries balanced with love and understanding.

With your partner, think about your expectations for the children, how you can apply consistent rules and boundaries, and how you can help them grow into respectful, responsible adults. At the same time, don't forget that the transition of entering a blended family can be pretty significant for some kids.

Remember why you're in a blended family. You chose your partner, knowing they have children and/or that you have children with someone else. With that may come some drama left over from former relationships. A partner with kids comes as a package deal and you'll have to contend with every part of that package—even if there are messy, complicated and stressful parts. Your role is to love and support and thus give your stepfamily the best chance for survival.

Letting Go

Your partner may come into your life with children, parents, ex-partners, friends and extended families, and they may not all accept you. But, if you prioritize finding ways to show love to your partner and your stepchildren, things will fall into place in due course. It is normal to be hurt, but you shouldn't remain wounded. Learn to drop it, leave it and let it go!

When you nurture ill feelings, you hurt yourself in the process. You kill your joy, and the resulting sadness adversely impacts the stepfamily and puts it on a downward spiral. Conversely, when you forgive and let go, you liberate yourself, carving the path to peace and joy in your family unit.

This attitude of holding on to past hurts creates a domino effect that negatively impacts every part of us—our spirit, emotions, thoughts, behaviors, physical body, and relationships. When there is unforgiveness, time stands still and wounds don't heal. Unforgiveness causes wounds to fester; it prolongs the pain. The longer we bear a grudge, the heavier the burden on our spirit becomes. Think of it like this: instead of pulling up and discarding the weeds of pain, we water and nurture them so they become fortified. In time they extract the nutrients from the surrounding support structure and we are rooted up with it—and just as a giant tree planted near a house grows and damages its foundation, so unforgiveness destabilizes our homes.

Develop strategies to handle issues once and for all and when they recur, correct them without resurrecting past failures. Some of your stepchild's actions will hurt indeed, but you must make an effort to let go, no matter how intensely you have been affected. It may take time to get over it, but time is a great healer. Unforgiveness will hurt the child and lead to physical and mental illness. In addition, it will cause ill feelings in the home and leave open sores that will be hard to heal.

I could not talk about forgiveness without mentioning forgiveness of your former partner if you have had a separation or divorce. You may have to forgive yourself and forgive your ex and his family. Forgiveness does not mean that you condone hurtful actions or that there should be no consequences for such actions. Forgiveness means that you let go of it. You let go of the feeling of wanting revenge for the pain you have suffered. It can take time, and you may have to work at it, but it can and must be done if you want to heal and find happiness.

Changing Faces

There is a saying that holding onto a grudge is like drinking poison and expecting another person to die from it. Unforgiveness creates stress, tension, bitterness, and anger—a deadly combination. Stress can cause physical, physiological, and emotional issues in your body. Juggling the demands of family life is stressful enough; there is no need to add the heaviness of unforgiveness to the mix. It affects your character—pain becomes your identity and steals your joy. Unforgiveness is like a trap, and when you fail to escape, you turn on yourself and others, and you become suspicious and cynical. In addition, research has shown that unforgiveness impairs the body's ability to heal and is a recipe for chronic pain, high blood pressure, a weakened immune system, reduced sleep, and cardiovascular problems.

Don't punish yourself for failures you had in your previous relationships. You can self-harm through actions like self-sabotage, seeking unhealthy coping mechanisms, speaking negatively to yourself, and letting yourself go.

Once you understand that you are not perfect and a work in progress, you will be well on your way to finding happiness. No one has it all together, and mistakes help us grow. If you are struggling to let go of those mistakes and continue to punish yourself, seek help from a counsellor.

Professionals can help you gain perspective and process your past. They can empower you to learn better ways to treat yourself and interact with others. Forgiving yourself will give you the freedom to thrive if you allow yourself to learn the lessons from your past and protect your heart.

Key points:

- When you fail to forgive, you hurt yourself in the process, and it is impossible to love others when you struggle to love yourself.

- You have the right to be hurt but not to remain wounded; learn to drop it, leave it, and let it go.

Chapter 4

NEPOTISM

One day we come to realize what's truly important in life. It's not money, the job, or stuff. It's people!

—*Andrea Campbell*

Children are generally resilient, and, despite the occasional bout of jealousy and sibling rivalry, they learn to share and get along with each other in time. Younger children are more likely to welcome a new brother or sister, especially those around the same age.

However, there are instances where children need more time to adapt to the new structure and may not be happy in their stepfamily. In addition, they may be contending with environmental and social pressures, which they may not have disclosed to their parents.

Nepotism rears its ugly head in all types of families. Parents can favor one biological child over another for many reasons, including gender, behavior, personality, and personal interests. Stepparents often favor their biological children over their stepchildren, which can cause various problems, including depression, low self-esteem, and lack of self-confidence later in a child's life.

The Pet Phenomenon

Unfortunately, some stepparents never emotionally connect with their stepchildren and may even treat them with hostility, resentment, and jealousy. If the new couple has a biological child together, often that child becomes the pet, and it is easy for the stepchild to feel isolated and unloved. This can cause long-term problems for the stepchild, who may demonstrate higher levels of aggression and poor performance in school. Some may describe this behavior as attention-seeking, but I do not doubt that there can be genuine hurt on the part of the child. Stepparents must take note of this behavior early and reassure the child.

Fairy tales throughout the ages have unfairly promulgated the concept of "the wicked stepmother", but we also have parents who are unkind to their biological or adopted children in equal measure. When a parent or stepparent overtly or covertly, intentionally or not, treats one of the children in the stepfamily less favorably than another, they are sowing discord in their family. It is like serving poison for dinner.

Nepotism

Parents often have favorites among their children. Sadly I have had first-hand experience of this, and I tell you in no uncertain terms, it was painful. I was the "outside" child, and I felt like an unwanted child! Although my mother was fair in supplying all my physical needs, she wasn't able to make me feel loved. As a result, I had a lot of fear, and my confidence was non-existent. As a result, I know from personal experience that nepotism also occurs unfavorably towards biological children; we mustn't assume it's always the stepchild who is mistreated.

Parents favor children based not only on bloodlines but also for other reasons—a child's perceived intelligence, ability, looks, and skin color. Therefore, biological parents and stepparents must be self-aware and vigilant to ensure they are not guilty of emotional abuse due to personal bias.

In my case, I felt that I was not my mother's biggest fan because I was close to my absent father. I looked forward to those weekends when he would visit, and I enjoyed our days out together. To add insult to injury, I physically resembled my dad and his family, so I was a constant reminder to my mother of her failed relationship with my father.

Your biological children may receive gifts from their grandparents and extended family while your stepchildren look on. There may be times when grandparents wish to take their grandchildren on vacation. Manage these dynamics so the stepchild does not feel left out of the equation. These are some of the external factors that may disrupt the harmony in the stepfamily. Stepparents must expect them to surface and develop strategies to mitigate any visible negative emotions.

I recognize that some things are out of your control, but there is always something you can do. For example, take the stepchild for a special treat when their stepsibling is away. Have a night in with them—watch a movie or play games. Reassure them that they are loved and explain that the grandparent loves them too but could not take them. Children do hurt, but they are more resilient than people think. Once they understand the dynamics, they are unlikely to hold resentment.

While you are developing relationships with your stepchildren, it's important to remember to continue to bond with your biological kids. You do not want to encourage or create an environment of jealousy in the home. Therefore, take care not to neglect your children as you juggle your new family.

Make time to spend with your biological children, whatever their age. Continue with your previous activities, like attending their school's sports day or watching your child perform in a concert. Make time to drop them off at their extracurricular activities and make that time count with interesting conversation. When you regularly give your child your undivided attention, it reminds them that they are important to you, despite all the changes in your home. With a larger family to support, you may work longer hours.

Whatever you do, make quality time for your children and stepchildren so that you can have a cohesive, happy home to go to at the end of the day.

Collateral Damage

Parental favoritism can damage relationships between stepsiblings and half-siblings. The siblings might compete for their parents' affection, or they might never really blend. Jealousy may set in, and they might never develop a close relationship. Open communication is an excellent way of addressing this problem. The sooner there is an open and honest dialogue about the feelings and struggles of those involved, the sooner the issue will be resolved.

Stepfamilies with a disabled child in their family unit must be particularly vigilant to ensure that they do not ignore the other children. It may be that they are not showing favoritism to the child with special needs, but they are more attentive to that child for obvious reasons. Other children in the family may feel that their mom or dad is less attentive to them because the disabled child demands so much more of their time. Always make time to reassure the other children and involve them in the care of their stepsiblings.

When you favor one child over another, it hurts the child who is left behind feeling unloved and affects the relationship that this child has with other children in the family. The stepchild might harbor ill feelings towards biological children, which may cause tension between them. Favoritism can be a huge obstacle for a child trying to assimilate into a stepfamily—making bonding almost impossible.

Some parents may not know that the favoritism they show to one child often hurts all the children, including the favorite or the pet, as some may call it. When siblings get on well, they do not want to see their sister or brother, biological or otherwise, being mistreated. It hurts the favored child, who often does not have the power or the courage to protest.

Far too many stepfamilies have experienced extreme and disturbing levels of preferential treatment. Stepparents must understand that all children crave love and attention and once they decide to be a stepparent, they must strive to meet this equitable universal hunger. For this to happen, stepparents must become very aware of the needs of each child and carefully consider how to engage with that child. Without a deliberate attempt to avoid nepotism, it is easy to isolate children and end up with somewhat inadvertent favoritism.

Key points:

- When you favor one child over another, it hurts the child who is left feeling unloved and affects the relationship that this child has with other children in the family.
- When siblings get on well, they do not want to see their sister or brother mistreated; it hurts the entire family.

Chapter 5

DEARTH

> A poverty mindset is not inherited; it is cultivated.
>
> —*Andrea Campbell*

Resources of any kind are not infinite. As a result, families find themselves making choices and often deny their children gadgets or other items that their hearts desire. Unfortunately, some parents and stepparents have adopted a scarcity mentality for no justifiable reason.

Many of us grew up in families where funds were genuinely scarce, and our parents had to make tough choices. Those were difficult days, and the skills we learned enabled us to manage our lives in an increasingly commerce-driven world. However, some people have adopted a poverty mindset as a default. They are trapped with the notion that they can hardly afford even the basics. As a result, they deny their children opportunities to pursue extracurricular activities—even when they occur in their local community. As a result, their children miss out on school outings and other events that would be wonderful experiences for them.

Some parents buy the cheapest brand of food available, and eating out is a rarity. They don't take holidays abroad and do not contribute to fundraising or charitable endeavors despite maintaining healthy bank accounts.

The absence of little luxuries and treats has very little to do with the family's disposable income. It is simply down to a deeply ingrained attitude of unaffordability irrespective of their bank balance. Some parents fail to release the shackles of the past, choosing instead to retain behaviors that used to be necessary for survival. And now that there are more resources, they cannot appreciate their improved circumstances. In most cases, the parents may not even be aware of the impact of their actions on their stepfamily.

The situation may become even more toxic if a family isolates itself, fearing the potential financial cost of entertaining people in their homes or attending social events. Consequently, their dearth experience generally goes unnoticed and remains unchallenged.

It is important to note that stepparents who demonstrate this attitude do not set out to hurt their stepchildren and endanger their stepfamilies. This is because, in their minds, they believe that they are taking the best course of action for their family. Some of these families are in custody battles or conflicts with their ex-partners—events that can harm the family's finances. The perception that their financial stability is threatened causes stepparents to keep a tight rein on their finances, securing them as if their lives depend on economic security.

The Scarcity Mindset

A scarcity mindset is the inherent feeling that there will never be enough. This leads to unproductive, unnecessary and self-defeating thoughts. A person with a scarcity mindset believes that opportunities are few and far between, so they must do all they can to hang on to what they have. This could not be further from the truth because new opportunities emerge constantly. When we adopt an abundance mindset, which I will discuss below, we position ourselves to grab these opportunities and capitalize on them.

Kids who grow up in scarcity suffer from the consequences throughout their lives. Child poverty can impact brain development, leading to mood disorders and substance abuse later in life. While stepfamilies with a scarcity mindset may not starve their children of food, they starve them of goods, services, and experiences that can enhance childhood happiness.

There may be, in fact, a positive side to maintaining a scarcity mentality. Parents prioritize their choices and focus on needs rather than wants. Scarcity focuses the mind on particular goals, ensuring that you effectively use what you have. Distractions are less tempting as you try to get more out of every dollar. However, this position must not be at the expense of a happy childhood.

The Concept of Money

Many of the preconceived notions we have about money are established during childhood. In some households, it isn't uncommon to hear parents say: "We don't have that kind of money," or "We can't afford that," even before they hear the price. This mindset can result in fear, anxiety, uncertainty about the future, and stress.

While it is necessary to avoid careless expenditure, it is also essential to have a family life. Your children are part of a wider community, and making them feel excluded augurs badly for a happy future.

Children don't have the maturity or experience to understand a constant sense of lack. Whatever their age, they need you to help them feel comfortable in their family unit. Avoid harping on how much things cost and how your family cannot afford them. That attitude does not inspire confidence and makes them worry about the future. They will become disgruntled if they feel their peers are leaving them behind.

Children must be taught life skills in an intentional and balanced way—including using money wisely and saving for the future. Parents can teach financial skills without denying their children opportunities to enjoy their childhood.

When your children introduce the idea of acquiring something, listen to them without judging or pressuring them to change their minds. Before saying, "We can't afford it", ask yourself, "Is this worth the expense?" That statement opens up the mind about what you can afford. If the item is unnecessary, find ways to teach your children the principles of choice, decision-making, and opportunity cost. Explain that they may have to forgo one thing for another because of financial pressures. But there is no need to live below your means intentionally. That attitude only curtails ambition as it directly courts a scarcity mindset. Instead of closing them down, teach your children to spend their time and energy in creating ways to have the means to access what they want from a mindset of abundance. Use powerful, positive words to empower and ignite an entrepreneurial and resourceful spirit in your children and stepchildren.

Additional Expenses

Families caring for children with special needs and disabilities generally have added expenses. These may consist of transportation costs, specialist equipment, special foods and clothing or the cost of care and therapy. Thankfully, the government has some financial benefits available to families caring for disabled or differently-abled children.

A quick search on the internet reveals various organizations that offer support in the form of grants for specific items or services. To begin, look at the Social Security Benefits for People with Disabilities website for the United States of America—www.ssa.gov/disability, where you can ascertain the various programs you can access for support. If you are in the United Kingdom, you can find information on government support at the website: www.gov.uk/browse/disabilities/benefits.

Whether you have a typical family or a stepfamily, finance is, for the most part, a challenging subject. However, every person incurs costs, and as parents and stepparents, we must do all we can to meet our children's needs and satisfy some of their wants. On the other hand, we shouldn't limit their life chances by curtailing their exposure to experiences that can enrich their lives and widen their knowledge and understanding of the world. It doesn't mean that you must spoil the children. Indeed this is not an either/or scenario. It is about striking the right balance within the scope of available resources to have a healthy family so the children can have great childhood memories.

An Abundance Mindset

The alternative to a scarcity mindset is an abundance mindset. When stepparents embrace an abundance mindset, they position themselves to have more choices and resources in their families. An abundance mindset states that there is plenty available for everyone. Achieving an abundance mindset requires a clear and present mind. It may not be an easy undertaking and will require patience and persistence, but working to shift from a scarcity mindset to one of abundance is worth the effort.

The first steps in developing an abundance mindset are recognizing that you have a scarcity mentality and then deciding that you want to adopt an abundance mindset. To succeed in your endeavor to make this shift, you must start making small sustainable changes in your parenting style and live a little. Please keep an open mind, and, instead of saying an outright "NO" when the stepchildren ask for something, use the opportunity to teach them life skills.

In developing an abundance mindset, you must be flexible and open to new opportunities. A scarcity mindset makes it difficult to embrace change because you focus on challenges rather than on opportunities.

An abundance mindset allows you to see things from a different perspective, and you will find better ways of achieving your goals. It does not mean you must exchange your core beliefs for others; you must be true to yourself throughout the process.

An abundance mindset requires a positive attitude; there is less focus on the negative aspects of your life and more on your aspirations. When you have an abundance mentality, you are happy to support others, and you will build relationships with your family members and with people wider afield. Those with a scarcity mentality miss out on this because they usually focus inwards rather than on other people's needs. A healthy balance must be pursued and achieved.

The cultural change from scarcity to abundance in your household is not dependent solely on you. However, it starts with you, so it depends largely on whether you have an abundance mindset in your family unit. What you think will determine if that happens.

Key points:

- Don't limit your children's life chances by curtailing their exposure to experiences that can enrich their lives and widen their knowledge and understanding of the world.

- The cultural change from scarcity to abundance in your household is not dependent solely on you, but it does start with you.

Chapter 6

ENNUI

Don't be surprised if people stop listening
if you are singing the same song all the time.

—*Andrea Campbell*

Sometimes, parents fall into such a routine that they find it difficult to break the monotony and have fun with their children. Their family runs like a well-oiled machine—very inflexible and highly predictable.

These families do not necessarily have financial issues; the parents may be tired, lethargic, or unmotivated. They think their life is exemplary, but the truth is they are bored, and so are the children. They are doing what needs to be done, but while it seems to be working on the surface, there is no soul in the family unit. The children have come to accept the status quo and turn to each other to find activities to cope with their boredom. They may also spend time online playing games but avoid physical and social interaction with their peers whom they think have more exciting lives. The children make the best of a bad situation and can emerge unscathed but with very few good memories to celebrate. Their self-confidence can also be damaged and take a long time to repair.

Some studies indicate that boredom is appropriate for children as it helps them develop their creativity and boosts their problem-solving skills. While there may be some credence to that, I can see no benefit in maintaining a mundane environment that hosts a boring family life. Your stepchild may be coming from a vibrant family environment where they had lots of choices. Should they find themselves in a joyless space, don't be surprised if they start to rebel.

Strategies for Tackling Boredom

A walk to the nearby park is a good start, but for this family, there is no time for that, or so they think. If mom or dad is ailing, the situation gets worse. The family sinks into a mundane lifestyle with no excitement, no surprises, and no joy. The routine becomes home-school-home. If they are religious, they may go to their place of worship one day per week and attend the occasional birthday party, but they will never be able to host their own party.

While you cannot entertain your children all the time, you must build activities into their lives that will challenge their minds or let them use their hands. These activities may include indoor and outdoor games, visits to places of interest, picnics, or other activities that will break the monotony.

A long list of activities may be possible for your stepfamily, depending on where you live. These include bird-watching, visiting museums, attending performances, playing music, painting, hiking, stamp collecting, among others. With so many choices available, it's difficult not to find something that a stepfamily will enjoy.

One game I like to play with my family is tree-hugging in the forest or the park. It is an exciting game that challenges their minds and improves their memory, imagination, and focus. This is a game played in pairs. One person is blindfolded and led to a random tree by a partner. With the blindfold on, the person is asked to familiarize him or herself with the tree by touching it, hugging it, feeling the roots, bark and other distinguishing features. That person is then led a distance away and the blindfold is removed. He or she is then asked to find the particular tree. This game could also be played using items in the home such as a set of different pens. On most occasions, the individual can find the tree or pen successfully, using senses apart from sight.

Thinking creatively is a sure way to beat boredom, but the inability to plan and follow through sometimes gets in the way.

The Beauty of Creativity

Stepparents can banish boredom quickly if they think creatively. If young children become bored with their toys, you might show them how to use them differently. For example, instead of building the same tower repeatedly, ask them to construct a farm by combining other toys. They may even be able to design a zoo. Ask them to consider which animals can cohabit and which ones will be at risk from the other. Let them build little stories in the process. Use craft supplies to decorate the dollhouse and get some new clothes for the doll. Use time at home with your stepchildren to nurture their curiosity.

Join in with your older children to build something worthwhile. For example, you could repurpose items around the house or items accessed from a thrift shop. But no matter how proactive you are, your activities won't fill your child's time for the entire day. Another idea is for them to write stories and draw pictures. They may stumble upon a new passion or hobby that could eventually become a side hustle. These activities build self-esteem and confidence while improving their creativity and entrepreneurship skills.

Children with ADHD and cognitive disabilities may find it harder to occupy themselves for long periods. Their attention spans and focus are usually shorter, so activities quickly lose their novelty and soon enough, they're off to the next activity. This is not the case for all children, though. For example, my daughter has Down syndrome and is happy to remain in one space and play with a single item for hours. Remember that each child is an individual, and you must get to know what your child likes and tailor your response accordingly. Do not copy what another family does; it may not work for your stepfamily.

If you look on the internet, you may be able to find outlets that offer disability-friendly activities and venues for your special child. Some of these venues are open to all the family and may even offer reduced rates for entry or use of space. In some regions, priority lines are available to children with disabilities and their families. From my experience, some airports will have a special line for people with disabilities and their families to make travel more achievable. So if you are keen to find opportunities to have fun, you will find them.

Whatever your situation, you must make time to have fun with your partner and the children. The stepfamily that plays together stays together.

Time for Love

Spend time alone as a couple. If a child needs special care in the family, ask a family member or a care professional for help. Make sure you have a care plan for whoever will care for your special child. Include everything the caregiver needs to know about them: contact details of relevant professionals, medications, special meals, favorite toys, meal times and other peculiarities. It may cost you money, but it's better to pay with money than pay with your peace of mind. When families unite into a blended family, life gets busy, and child-free time is easily neglected.

Set aside time at regular intervals to do something you and your partner enjoy without the children involved. It may be a simple act such as visiting your favorite beauty spot, going to the movies, or eating out. Date nights and time away from the children are suitable for your family as they give you and your partner the chance to reconnect, ease tensions, and make plans. It's an excellent opportunity to discuss family issues and talk about anything. It provides a chance to recharge, refresh, and renew your love for each other and the children in your stepfamily.

A famous saying, "All work and no play makes Jack a dull boy," is pertinent here. My mom may not always have been kind to me, but we could always look forward to a family outing during the school holidays. Families must understand that, even with limitations, they must find ways to have fun and build surprises that engender joy in the family unit.

Key points:
- Families must understand that even if there are limitations, they must find ways to have fun and build surprises that inspire joy in the family unit.
- You may have to spend money for the privilege, but it's better to spend money than to sacrifice your peace of mind.

Chapter 7

RETICENCE

Peace and silence are not synonymous
—*Andrea Campbell*

Effective communication in the blended family increases trust between family members. Open, transparent, and frequent communication reduces misunderstanding and improves the connection between parents, among siblings, and between parents and stepchildren. Conversely, when there is a breakdown of communication, one of the parties shuts down. This behavior damages the stepfamily and encourages people to harbor grudges.

It is very damaging when a stepparent stonewalls or engages in silent treatment towards a child. Withdrawing interaction or refusing to engage with the child threatens the stepfamily's health. The technique can be used to avoid conflict, but it can also be used to exercise control and inflict punishment. The children experience depression and anxiety, and feel unloved and rejected when it happens. It is manipulative and punishing when you exclude or ignore people or give them the cold shoulder or the silent treatment. In essence, you are inflicting emotional or physical harm—a decision over which you have a choice. My mother often used this technique when she argued with my stepfather. Though it was not targeted at the children in the household, it caused the environment to have an unwelcome heaviness, essentially squeezing the joy out of the home.

When Silence isn't Golden

One of the idioms I learned as a child is, "Silence is golden". My parents used that saying to keep the children quiet during a period when they believed that children were to be seen and not heard. Happily, that era has passed, and now everyone has a voice for the most part.

The silent treatment is often triggered when one partner pressures or overwhelms the other with requests, criticism, or complaints. The receiver then responds with silence and emotional and social distance. Giving the silent treatment is of no benefit to the person who has withdrawn. On the contrary, it shows that the individual is consumed by anger and lacking self-control. This behavior creates a significant imbalance with the child and the stepfamily.

While silence or a pause can be used briefly, with an appropriate explanation such as, "I need a minute," to cool tempers after a heated exchange, it is when silence is used as a deliberate strategy to inflict pain and exercise control that it creates a problem. That strategy is never acceptable and is, in fact, damaging. Stepparents may resort to this for a short period to avoid utterings they may regret later. In this case, it is excusable.

Passive aggression is a real phenomenon. Sarcasm, procrastination, sullenness, sabotage, backhanded compliments, spite, and nit-picking are ways that people express aggression indirectly, sometimes without even realizing it. It is not enough to avoid conflict; it is also important to actively address it as it arises. It is incredibly unhealthy for one party to bottle up feelings of resentment in a family.

Maintaining silence for fear of relationship breakdown or avoiding hurting another person's feelings has the exact opposite effect. Not expressing your feelings hurts the other person because they will know something is wrong and may not even know what it is. When our children display the same behavior it hurts us, so why would it not hurt them when we do it? We all understand the importance of good communication in families, but often we ignore this, holding back as we resort to silence.

Communication Woes

The phenomenon of silence is more prevalent in families where the power dynamics are out of balance and one party feels they have more to lose if they cause the other to be angry.

It does not take much to get overwhelmed by your blended family structure, especially if a custody battle is in progress. Try to comprehend the situation and do your best under the circumstances. Often your anger is not brought about by members of your stepfamily but by people attached to the family—an absent parent or former in-laws. It is easy to go quiet to avoid unleashing your anger onto your stepfamily when this occurs.

If, for example, you find that you are fighting with your ex and this is disturbing your peace, try harder to work things out with the absent parent to reduce your stress level and achieve peace of mind. You may have to make concessions. When you stop seeing your former partner as an enemy and instead try to work with them, it makes things easier for all involved.

I used to be amid conflicts between my parents when my dad visited and wanted to take me out for the day. My mother hated that idea, and she always rebelled. I felt confused when my dad told me to get ready while my mom commanded me to stay put. My dad usually won, but I felt my mother took her revenge on me when I returned home. She often gave me the silent treatment. When she did speak, it was to order me around.

It is necessary to find the right balance between reticence and speaking out. Silence has a place in communication, for in any healthy relationship, parties take turns listening. However, if there are issues to be addressed, prolonged silence is not an appropriate approach to take.

Effective communication is not just about exchanging information. It's about understanding the emotions and intentions behind the information. Not only do you need to convey a message clearly, but you also need to do some active listening to obtain the true meaning of what's being said and be better able to respond in turn. When you learn these skills, you will deepen your connections with your stepfamily and thus build greater trust and respect. This will allow you to work together to improve the well-being of your family.

Words have relevance, but they are not the sole means of communicating with your stepfamily. Your body language and ability to be there for them are equally relevant. Effective communication helps build strong connections between blended family members. Stepfamilies must spend time together and openly address issues that cause conflict. Solid, well-functioning stepfamilies employ various communication methods to interact with one another. They do not resort to silence; instead, they work to build nurturing relationships by treating each other with respect and consideration. They take opportunities to share, whether at the dining table, in the family room, or in their cars. They communicate with their voice and gestures, paying attention to body language and tone of voice as much as they do to the words they choose to use.

Parents must create opportunities for addressing burning issues in an open and non-judgmental atmosphere conducive to listening and learning. When families have fun together, this environment creates opportunities for open communication, and one subject can lead to another. However, if you are seriously aggrieved, try discussing it with your partner first in a calm private space, not when you are angry.

As reticence between the parents is tremendously damaging to relationships, it is in their best interest to avoid it. Failure to do so adversely impacts the relationship satisfaction for both parents reduces feelings of intimacy and reduces the capacity to keep the family in a healthy and wholesome space. Moreover, continued failure to address issues will lead the family into a downward spiral and into an abyss they may never be able to escape.

Key points:
- It is not enough to avoid conflict; it is also important to actively address it as it arises.
- Parents owe it to their children to maintain a peaceful environment in their home.
- Resorting to silence is damaging to relationships in the stepfamily.

CONCLUSION

When all is said and done, stepparents are responsible for protecting and caring for the children in their family unit. A man or woman who truly loves their partner will also make every effort to love their stepchildren. Love, however, is a strong word for some people. Nineteenth Century British writer C.S. Lewis once said, "Do not waste time bothering whether you 'love' your neighbor; act as if you did. As soon as we do this we find one of the great secrets. When you are behaving as if you loved someone, you will presently come to love him. If you injure someone you dislike, you will find yourself disliking him more." Sometimes love can be a choice before it is a feeling.

If you find it hard to love your stepchild, the reason may not be because they are not yours biologically; it may just be that your personalities clash or there are other dynamics at play. The child may be misbehaving because they miss their absent parent, blame you for the breakup, or simply be having a hard time processing all the changes. When this happens, do not attempt to fight fire with fire.

Instead, you must use water to extinguish the fire—don't stoke it or add more fuel by implementing more rules or engaging in a power struggle.

Many of us focus too heavily on the fact that the child is not ours biologically. We tend to forget that biological children also create challenges for their parents. Every parent can recall moments of unhappiness with the behavior of a biological child. I acknowledge that the dynamics change when it's not your child, but sometimes the challenges do not stem from the stepparent relationship. It is simply a child being mischievous as children often are.

Allocate sufficient resources to nurture your stepfamily. Do not deny the children opportunities to engage in extracurricular activities; get in there with them when possible. Adopt an attitude of gratitude and an abundance mindset. Use every chance to teach and inspire your stepchildren to develop life skills and position them for their lives. You will incur additional costs if there is a special child in your family. Conduct research to identify resources available to lessen the impact on your stepfamily.

Only love can conquer hate. Though it requires patience, achieving a happy home is often worth the effort. There is no need to prove anything to a child; be confident in who you are and be the best stepparent possible. Allow your biological children to interact normally with their stepsiblings. Remember, your ultimate goal is to have a happy home. You don't

Conclusion

want to live a life filled with drama. Your home should be your safe space; do all you can to preserve it.

Once you are secure in who you are, there is no need to engage in petty fights with children. You are the master of your destiny, and you should not allow anyone to make you fight for what you already know you have or who you are. Protect your heart by avoiding unnecessary conflict and discord in your home. Entertain neither superiority nor inferiority complex.

Do not expect everyone else to love you, but do love yourself. Low self-esteem can wreck the human spirit and cause you to repel opportunities for love and light. Your future is in your hands. Handle it with care. Embrace your responsibility to raise the next generation—a generation of individuals who will become masters of their destinies.

So there you have it—seven unsuspecting attitudes that are seriously toxic to stepfamilies. Bureaucracy, lambasting, unforgiveness, nepotism, dearth, ennui and reticence are joy killers. They must be kept far from your stepfamily if you expect to achieve that happy, wholesome life you desire and deserve.

Once you have considered and reflected upon your actions concerning the seven elements introduced in this book, let go of any feelings of inadequacy or anger. There is no panacea for building a successful stepfamily, but if you can look in the mirror and honestly say that you have done your best, that is an accomplishment of which you can be proud. Continue to strive for joy in your household—the family that laughs together will stay together. Time is a great healer; make it your ally and be at peace with yourself and others. Treasure each moment, and do not allow the storms of life to blow your house down. Hold on to love and light and know that these too shall pass.

REMINDER

We hope you enjoyed this text.

Please remember to leave a review if you bought this book online. Also, please note that if you purchased the text in a physical store or received the book as a gift, you can still leave a review on Amazon.

Thank you for acquiring this book and thanks on behalf of the families who will benefit from your support.

Other Books You'll Love

https://amzn.to/3q8nO7F

    The 9-L model illustrated in "Blended and Special" explores the dynamics of stepfamilies caring for children with special needs and disabilities and presents the information in digestible nuggets ready for consumption by quintessential blended families juggling the demands of parenthood with caring for children with special needs.

    Whether you have an established stepfamily or are in the early stages of a blended family, you can find value in the information presented

    Also included is a chapter of real-life case studies from stepparents caring for disabled children. The experiences they share hold valuable lessons on issues that may arise and how they handled them in their endeavor to maintain a happy stepfamily.

https://amzn.to/3oyhBIh

The Pocket Learner is an educational system the author initially developed to help her child with special educational needs. The system became an international multi-award-winning innovation and has been extended to families across the globe to help their children build vocabulary, learn to read, and count.

The toolkit covers the roles, responsibilities, and activities that families and other relevant parties must implement.

The framework revolves around the child, the star in the center and the fruit of the womb, endowed with innate abilities and gifts to share with the world. It advocates early and consistent intervention by the relevant parties and promotes collaboration among a range of services and the child's family. This synergetic strategy is an aspiration that, if achieved, yields optimum results for your special child.

https://amzn.to/3AUCH06

As our world gets busier, we are inundated with the complexities of life, and as we grow up, we forget to play and have fun. Life Lessons from a Bouncing Ball is a much-needed reminder that play is not just for kids. Apart from stimulating joy and enhancing relaxation, play boosts our creativity and imagination and positively impacts our relationships and personal success.

The importance of play for children is well documented. Now researchers have turned their attention to its possible benefits for adults. They're finding that play isn't just about having fun; it can also be an important means of reducing stress and enhancing our overall well-being.

Personal success is subjective and ever-changing. You can learn lessons through play even if you think you don't know how to play. The strategies are creative and can be adapted, even if you are playing alone. After reading this book, you'll never look at play in the same way again.

RESOURCES

Abraham, K., Studaker-Cordner, M., (n.d.). *Stepchildren Making You Crazy? 5 Ways to Manage Conflict in Blended Families.* Empowering Parents.Com. Retrieved March 16, 2022, from https://www.empoweringparents.com/article/stepchildren-making-you-crazy-5-ways-to-manage-conflict-in-blended-families/

Benefits for People with Disabilities. (n.d.). Social Security. Retrieved March 15, 2022, fr. https://www.ssa.gov/disability

Canda. (2020, June 6). *Forgiveness in Second Marriages.* Blended Restoration. Retrieved March 15, 2022, from http://blendedrestoration.com/forgiveness-in-second-marriages/

Effective communication is the key to blended family success. (n.d.). Blended and Stepfamily Resource Centre. Retrieved March 16, 2022, from https://blendedfamilyadvice.com/effective-communication-is-the-key-to-blended-family-success/

Henry, J. (n.d.). *Family Dynamics.* Https://Irp-Cdn.Multiscreensite.Com. Retrieved March 16, 2022, from https://irp-cdn.multiscreensite.com/6887d51e/files/uploaded/john-henry-psychologist-Family%20Dynamics.pdf

Mere Christianity. (n.d.). PBS. Retrieved July 11, 2022, from https://www.pbs.org/wgbh/questionofgod/ownwords/mere2. html)

Miller, G. (n.d.). *The Benefits of Boredom.* The Child Mind Institute. Retrieved March 16, 2022, from https://childmind.org/article/the-benefits-of-boredom/

Rowett, A. (2015, April 14). *The Prison of Unforgiveness.* Bellevue Christian. Retrieved March 16, 2022, from https://bellevuechristiancounseling.com/articles/the-prison-of-unforgiveness

Scott, K. (n.d.). *The effects of the silent treatment in families and relationships.* ABC Everyday. Retrieved March 16, 2022, from https://www.abc.net.au/everyday/the-effect-of-silent-treatment-in-relationships-families/11059348

ABOUT THE AUTHOR

Andrea Campbell, MBA, MA is a social entrepreneur, linguist, and inspirational writer. Since publishing her first business book in 2010, Andrea has released several inspirational books and articles about special needs parenting and personal development, including two Amazon No. 1 bestsellers.

Over the years, she has focused on empowering vulnerable people through education and inspiration. As the mother of a child with special educational needs, she is particularly keen on working with families to enable their disabled children to aspire higher and achieve their potential. She is also the inventor of the Pocket Learner – a set of innovative educational resources for parents, caregivers and educators of children with special educational needs.

Andrea has also published various inspirational coloring books, journals and activity books to empower and inspire people everywhere.

Andrea resides with her family in London, UK, where she continues to positively impact through her writing, creative exploits, training programs, coaching, philanthropy, and inspirational speaking.

Printed in Great Britain
by Amazon